SILENT CONVERSATION

CLAIRE ELIZABETH GROSE

Copyright © 2021 by Claire Elizabeth Grose

Compiled and edited by Michael Grose and June Kennedy

All rights reserved. No portion of this publication may be reproduced, stored in a retrieval system or transmitted in any form by any means – electronic, mechanical, photocopying, recording, or any other –except for brief quotation in printed reviews, without the prior written permission of the publisher.

Unless indicated otherwise, all scripture quotations in this book are from the following source:

The Good News Bible: The Bible in Today's English Version (TEV) © 1976 by the American Bible Society. Used with permission.

ISBN 978-0-6486884-4-0

Author contact information - clairegrose.heartmatters@gmail.com

Version 1.0

DEDICATION

This book is dedicated to Gloria and Jim
My beloved sister and brother-in-law

CONTENTS

DEDICATION IV

CONTENTS V

PREFACE VIII

ACKNOWLEDGEMENTS X

   PART ONE 1

      MY DAILY PRAYER 4

      MISTY MOON 5

      A SIMPLE THING 6

      FIND A PLACE OF BEAUTY 7

      A LAPPING TIDE 8

      WAITING FOR DAWN 9

      FIND HIM IN THE GARDEN 10

      A WARDROBE OF SEASONS 11

      BOUNTY OF BEAUTY 14

      GARDEN SOLACE 15

      HALO OF FLOWERS 16

      INNER REST 17

      STANDING ON THE BEACH 18

      MOUNTAIN TOP MOMENTS 19

      MOTHER NATURE'S DESIGNS 20

      MOONLIGHT 21

      MORNING MELODIES 22

      FLOWERS BRING HEALING 23

      ABOVE THE BLUE 26

      SHARE YOUR HEART WITH THE SAVIOUR 27

      LOOK TO THE SKY 28

      LEAD ME ON TO VICTORY 29

   PART TWO 30

      SILENT CONVERSATION 33

      UNSPOKEN PEACE 34

      MY COMPASS 35

      OPEN HIS WORD 36

PEACE OF MIND	37
PAGES OF HOPE	38
MY GREAT HEALER	41
HIS WORD WILL LIFT YOU UP	42
HE CARES FOR YOU	43
HIS LOVE IS ALL I KNOW	44
GUIDE ME	45
FACE EACH DAY	46
FEED YOUR FAITH	49
HOLY SPIRIT LOVE	50
REFLECTION	51
HIS GREATEST BLESSING	52
MY QUIET TIME	53
FORGIVE TO RECEIVE	54
GLIMPSE OF HOPE	57
RAINBOW'S WONDER	58
SHOW HIS LOVE	59
LOVE AND GRACE FOR ALL	60
COVER ME WITH YOUR WINGS	61
HIS QUIET VOICE	62
RICH IN CHRIST	63
BOW AT HIS THRONE	64
THE TWISTS AND TURNS OF LIFE	65
HEALING BALM	66
TWO BECOME ONE	67
ETERNAL SPRING	68
PART THREE	69
A SPECIAL PURPOSE	72
SPEAK TO MY SOUL LORD	73
HIS WILL BE DONE	74
ALL IN HIS APPOINTED TIME	75
ASK	76
STRENGTH TO BE HAPPY	77
WHAT'S BEST FOR ME	80
PEARLS OF LIGHT	81

YOUR LOVE, MY LOVE	82
YOUR WORDS	83
THE SACRED SOUL	84
TRUST, FAITH AND BELIEF	85
PART FOUR	86
IN THE SHADOWS OF THE OLIVE GROVE	89
EASTER LOVE	90
PIERCED HANDS	91
THANK YOU FOR CALVARY	94
HOLY SPIRIT	95
A PRICELESS LIFE	98
THIS BABY BOY	99
ANGELS BROUGHT JOY	100
STAR OF THE EAST	101

PREFACE

Two things I just wanted to say about this book are, why I started writing and how I came by the title.

I grew up in the 1950's-1960's in Adelaide, South Australia, my life was pretty simple but wonderful. I was very lucky to have a secure family life, and my Mum and Dad brought the family up to treat others with respect, do the right thing, be courteous and respect your elders. We had a strict upbringing and even as adults our parents never criticized us but encouraged us to do our best in life. They were "Aussie battlers" but we always managed to make it through the tough times!

They were people of integrity and cared about others and instilled that into our family.

Church was a big part of our lives growing up. We went to Sunday School at an early age and progressed up through the appropriate groups as we got older.

Youth groups, camps and church anniversaries were all important to the whole family. We competed in church sports teams, basketball and tennis with other parishes across Adelaide. Life-long friendships were in the making and cherished golden memories to look back on that would never fade.

Bible stories, hymns and choruses were all part of getting to know Jesus. This nurturing finally led me to the day Jesus came knocking on my heart's door. Being filled with the Holy Spirit is something I will never forget and the overwhelming power of His love that filled my whole being and propelled me to the front of the hall to give my heart to Him. No words can fully describe the joy I felt. That was in February 1968, I was 14 years of age. He has been my Shining Light ever since, and lives within me always.

So I thank my beautiful Mum and Dad for the way they raised me and for the foundation of knowing Jesus' love.

SILENT CONVERSATION

It was in His love that I started to write, in the autumn of 1993. My journey has brought me to this book "Silent Conversation", which is prayer time with God. No one else knows or sees into your heart , only God and it is there you can share all your needs and cares in your life. You can pray anytime and anywhere knowing your prayer is heard by God Himself!

"When you pray, he will answer you, and you will keep the vows you made." Job 22:27 Good News Bible

When preparing this book, I found various scripture references that spoke of His love for us and how He wants us to stay in touch with Him in every detail of our lives.

When I was a young Christian reading my Bible was really important to me in getting to know Jesus as my personal Saviour and became the foundation that I built my faith on.

It gave me strength and courage as I began life in the workforce at the age of 16. Coming from a sheltered upbringing it was my life-line to self-confidence and adapting to social life at work.
The poems reflect the everyday feelings and emotions that we feel as we meet the challenges of life and how the great magnitude of God's love can help us rise above them.

I pray you will seek His eternal counsel in your everyday life and receive His grace and mercy in "Silent Conversation".

Many of these writings have been my first words of whispered prayer, so much that I have been moved to write them down at once and continue on in His wonderful and absolute love.

Together we write as He provides my inspiration.

All glory to Him, my precious Lord Jesus!

ACKNOWLEDGEMENTS

My heartfelt thanks to my beloved family, my Mum and Dad, Lilly and Kenny, and my siblings Jeanette, June, Carol, Gloria and Lynne, for their never ending encouragement and support to me. To the rest of the family, you are all a precious link that joins us together.

To Michael and Andrew for your continual support to me in fulfilling my passion of writing poems for the Lord to help others through His Word.

A huge thank you to Junie for editing my poems and the coffees and lunches we enjoyed along the way.

To Joy Furnell for her Crown of Thorns drawing, you have an amazing gift, thank you Joy.

Special thanks to Salisbury Uniting Church Adelaide, for the cover photograph and stained glass window photo. Used by permission.

To my friends and Church Families, thank you for your love and support.

To my beautiful sons, Michael and Andrew, your Partners and my Grandchildren. I thank my precious Lord Jesus for giving you all to me and I will love you forever.

To you the reader, thank you for picking this book up and I pray you will find His peace and love on the pages ahead.

May He shower you all with His love and blessings.

PART ONE

"I love you just as the Father loves me;
Remain in my love."

John 15 : 9

SILENT CONVERSATION

TAKE TIME TO REFLECT…

"You will show me the path that leads to life; your presence fills me with joy and brings me pleasure forever."

Psalm 16 : 11

MY DAILY PRAYER

Be with me, stay with me,
Close by my side,
Fill me with Your peace and love,
So my spirit shall surely fly
To the heights in Your love,
As only You can give,
Prepare me for this day ahead,
So in me You'll always live.

MISTY MOON

Misty moon in the sky
On a winter's night,
Waiting for the haze to pass
To shine her light so bright.

Softly she hangs up there
To mark the end of day,
Stars begin to shine,
We see the Milky Way.

Misty moon sits patiently
To pass the night away,
Designed by the Saviour
He sends her on her way.

Misty moon so silent
Still speaks a thousand words,
Melts my heart completely
When she shows her perfect curves!

A SIMPLE THING

I saw something special,
An autumn leaf upon its side,
Rolling along like a wagon wheel,
Forced by the wind behind.

Nothing could stop this motion,
Rolling along at full speed,
Such a simple thing
Was royalty to me!

The simple things of life
That Mother Nature provides,
They bring their joy for sure
But only come along sometimes.

So thank you Lord, for the simple things
That bring their peace and calm,
When we take the time
To see things for what they are.

FIND A PLACE OF BEAUTY

A waterfall refreshing,
Majestic, graceful and cool,
Misty spray floats in the air,
Cascades into a pool.

Birds eye views from mountain tops
As far as the eye can see,
This world You created Lord
Still brings joy to me.

On a foggy day the sea lies flat,
Such calm reigns supreme,
Time seems to stand still,
A view you cannot see.

Valleys green so glorious,
Lush with blooms and trees,
Touch my heart in wonder,
Your beauty I can see.

The wonder of Your creation,
What peace it brings to me,
Finding a place of beauty
Is what we truly need.

A LAPPING TIDE

When I hear a lapping tide
I think Lord of You,
Walking on the water
As only You can do.

The tide is slow and gentle,
Murmurs rhythmically
Beating the shore,
I feel You come to me.

Just like two thousand years ago
When You walked on the sea,
Wonder filled the hearts of those
On the shores of Galilee.

WAITING FOR DAWN

The air is crisp and clear,
Darkness all around,
Stars seem oh so near
But their place is heaven bound.

Coolness wraps around me,
No warmth to be found,
Quiet reigns supreme,
There's not a single sound.

I'm waiting for dawn to come,
This winter seems so deep,
Can't wait for the sun to rise
While I try to get some sleep.

Soon first light appears
The horizon comes to life,
Heralding the day,
Thank You Lord it's end of night.

FIND HIM IN THE GARDEN

Find Him in the morning
When day is fresh and new,
Misty clouds rise to the heights,
Morning melodies greet Him too.

Find Him in the morning
When dawn crowns the sky,
Before thoughts fill your mind,
He's right there by your side.

Find Him in the garden
While the leaves are wet with dew,
A place of peace and comfort
To help you feel renewed.

Your heart and soul will be refreshed
As you go through your day,
The Lord is waiting patiently
To help in a special way!

A WARDROBE OF SEASONS

Earth revolves in space,
Sun and moon play their part,
What a glorious creation
The Saviour set her path.

Mother Nature is in tune,
A fresh dawn arrives,
Pushing through another day,
Sunset bows on time.

She is dressed in seasons,
Summer, Autumn, Winter and Spring,
The calendar unfolds,
Ever changing weather she brings.

Her wardrobe is ever changing,
In the colours of the rainbow,
Her beauty is around us,
She displays a mighty show.

In awe and in wonder
We gaze at the world,
On the day we meet the Saviour,
How He made it, He will tell.

HE WILL REFRESH YOU EVERYDAY…

"Fill us each morning with your constant love,
so that we may sing and be glad all our life."

Psalm 90 : 14

BOUNTY OF BEAUTY

Bounty of beauty
Found on Mother Earth,
Lord, you filled her with treasure
So the world she could serve.

Earth's bounty of beauty,
All our needs she gives,
We only have to find them,
Her treasure lies within.

Bounty of beauty
All over the land,
Below and above the earth
Such treasure by His hand.

The wealth He supplies
Is a treasure indeed,
To serve mankind,
For all that he needs.

GARDEN SOLACE

You never have to look far
For the beauty of God's love,
It's usually in your garden,
It's flowers, leaves and buds.

Tightly packed within each case,
Beauty waits to unfold,
At His appointed time
Sweet buds you can behold.

Look to His garden for solace,
You'll surely find it there,
Serenity and wonder
Will lift your every care!

HALO OF FLOWERS

Halo of love made by Him
In perfect colours divine,
Mother Nature's gardens
Are born time after time.

She blends them all together
In perfect harmony,
To give us joy and wonder
To smell, touch and see.

She sends her rains to fall
To refresh and beckon growth,
For new buds to appear,
The time I love the most.

So thank You Lord for flowers
Made by Your holy hand,
Exquisite style to delight the soul,
They bloom on Your command.

INNER REST

When I look at the sea
I feel You speak to me,
Calmness flows through me,
In love I praise Thee.

The sun shining on the sea
Like diamonds flashing bright,
Restores my heart and soul,
Your presence comes to light.

I feel You near to me,
My thoughts are of Thee,
The King of Kings in glory,
Bright as bright can be.

So for peace and calm to own you,
Watch a sunrise or sunset,
His glory shining bright,
Will bring you inner rest.

STANDING ON THE BEACH

When I walk on the beach
And watch the waves come to shore,
I think of You Lord
Where You stood centuries before.

You felt the same breeze
And the sun upon Your face,
You saw every dawn
And every sunset You embraced.

The seasons of time
Roll over each year,
Standing on the beach Lord
Brings You near.

So when next you walk
On the open beach
Spare a thought for the Saviour,
The same breeze you will meet.

MOUNTAIN TOP MOMENTS

Mountain top moments
Are when I meet with You,
Your sparkling waters
Come into view.

Mountain top moments
Your Spirit I find,
Brings me great joy
Time after time.

Mountain top moments
Shine the most,
Reflecting on them
I feel You close.

There are still steep climbs
Sure enough that's true,
But mountain top moments
Give the greatest view.

MOTHER NATURE'S DESIGNS

Look to mother nature
For colour, shape and design,
She has years of experience
Through the centuries of time.

Just like human nature
She has royalty and class,
Leaders and followers,
Some command and others ask.

Her majesty in colour
We can never compete,
From the smallest to the biggest,
Her designs we'll never beat.

Then it comes to her structures,
How magnificent they stand,
Only the Lord Almighty
Could create them from His hands.

So look to mother nature,
She has the answers true,
But God's most special creation
In His eyes is you!

MOONLIGHT

Here she comes lighting up the sky,
This ball of light,
His glorious moon sits above
As the world drifts on by.

There's something about the moon
We all love to watch,
She sends nourishing vibes
That make us want to stop.

Her warming light so pleasing
From her lofty place,
She can light up earth
From her position in space.

Yes there's something about moonlight
From her place up there,
The peace she brings to our soul,
Makes us forget our cares.

MORNING MELODIES

Morning melodies greet the dawn,
What sweet joy the birds bring
When saluting the sunrise,
Singing to the King.

The noise can be so deafening
In the forest so deep,
Or quiet symphonies
In the pines by the sea.

Where ever you are at the break of dawn,
Beautiful choruses you will find,
Always there to greet the morn,
Morning melodies chime on time.

FLOWERS BRING HEALING

Soft, delicate and pure,
Raised by His holy hand
From the place He made the stars,
So elegantly they stand.

Flowers bring such healing
To the heart and soul,
In sadness or in joy,
Unspoken words are told.

Their colours are unique,
A rainbow to reveal,
Small or large a wonder,
A weeping heart they will heal.

SILENT CONVERSATION

GOD IS FAITHFUL…

"He is near to those who call to him,
who call to him with sincerity."

Psalm 145 : 18

ABOVE THE BLUE

You wait endlessly
For my heart to share
What lies within,
As I say my daily prayers.

We sort things out You and I,
Heartfelt dreams I give to You,
My future You already know,
Trust is all I have to do.

My whispered prayers I offer You,
Drift on high above the blue
Into Your loving care
Where You sort them through.

So thank you Lord for loving me
And waiting for me endlessly,
Above the blue for all my prayers
And all things I share with Thee.

SHARE YOUR HEART WITH THE SAVIOUR

One thing I know Lord,
Everything has a reason,
The time and the place,
Like every changing season.

Life's changing situations
Sometimes bring us to our knees,
It's there we meet Jesus,
Into our heart He can see.

He wants to celebrate
Our joys with us,
Go to Him for everything
Use your faith and trust.

Treat Him like a friend,
Share your ups and downs,
Take everything to the Saviour,
Each prayer is glory bound.

LOOK TO THE SKY

Look to the sky for courage,
Heaven lies beyond,
The Saviour in His glory,
His care I rely upon.

Look to the sky for strength
When life is heavy to bear,
The Master is always with you,
Just ask Him and He is there.

Look to the sky for hope,
Your dreams He'll share with you,
Your whispers are always heard,
He always cares for you.

So look to the sky for love,
Eternal it will always be,
The King of Kings is yours,
We are together, His family.

LEAD ME ON TO VICTORY

Help me to have a light step Lord
As I pass through each day,
Confident in Your love
That's with me to stay.

Help me to have a light step
When challenges come along,
In prayer I hand them to You,
It's then You make me strong.

I ask for Your strength
And Your will to come to pass,
Even my smallest worry
Becomes your most loved task!

So thank You precious Lord
For the faith You've given me,
I'm so glad You are mine,
Lead me on to victory.

PART TWO

"…Happy are those who put
their trust in the Lord."

Isaiah 30 : 18

LEAVE YOUR PRAYERS…
IN HIS HANDS…

"If you believe, you will receive
whatever you ask for in prayer."

Matthew 21 : 22

SILENT CONVERSATION

In silent conversation Lord
My thoughts run to You,
Without a spoken word
That You already knew.

In silent conversation
You know my heart's desire,
Your plan will prevail
No matter what betides.

In silent conversation
No words are exchanged,
Your thoughts, my thoughts
Are linked like a chain.

In silent conversation
Your prompts come to me,
I praise and worship You Lord,
In my heart You'll always be.

UNSPOKEN PEACE

Thank You Lord for Your love that brings
Your peace to me in simple things,
Like watching the rain on a winter's day
Or autumn leaves rolling on their way.

Thank You Lord for a gentle lapping tide,
With diamonds dancing on the waves
They make their way to shore,
A journey they take every day.

Pure solace on a mountain top,
Unspoken peace comes to me,
A setting sun that makes me stop,
Musky pinks and purples I see.

A full moon in its place
Can melt a heart that's true,
Unspoken peace comes to me
To restore my faith in You.

MY COMPASS

I'm heading into the unknown,
My path is veiled from me,
But I must keep moving forward,
Blue skies I want to see.

My compass will lead me on,
The Lord directs my path,
He will be my shield
And help me with each task.

My compass has a light
That shines forever more,
Guiding my feet and heart
For what's in store.

My compass is the Lord Almighty,
In Him I put my trust,
Lover of my soul,
Follow Him I must.

OPEN HIS WORD

You can open His Word
To hear Him speak,
Straight to your heart
When you're feeling weak.

He loves you so much,
That He wants to bear
The weight you can't carry,
That's why you must share.

Open His Word for calm and peace,
His healing and strength you will find,
Open His Word to receive His love
And His mercy and grace every time.

PEACE OF MIND

I lay my heart at Your feet,
Not knowing what lies ahead,
Your plans for me I seek,
My concerns I want to shed.

In my prayers I seek answers
As each one comes to light,
Safely in Your hands,
I believe You will provide.

Give me Your strength of mind
So I will always find
Complete peace to live
In Your guiding light.

So thank You Lord for peace of mind,
Knowing You are in control,
Though challenges keep rising up,
My problems You will solve.

PAGES OF HOPE

The fragile heart it trembles,
The pain is just too much
When the road you are travelling
Is no longer smooth but rough.

Changes must be made,
Utter a desperate prayer,
Never give up on hope,
The Saviour is always there.

Turn to His pages of hope,
You will find the strength to bear,
The Holy Bible is truly a manual
Over centuries of time have been shared.

He speaks to those who are hurting,
And to those with joy to share,
His promises are forever,
For you, He honestly cares!

YOUR ARMS REACH FOR ME…
NO MATTER HOW FAR…

"Whenever I am anxious and worried,
you comfort me and make me glad".

Psalm 94 : 19

MY GREAT HEALER

You are my great healer,
When I call You to my side
Nothing can come between us,
The love we share You and I.

There I find Your pure love,
I'm so glad You are mine,
When earth's cares weigh me down,
Your Throne I have to find.

You are my great healer
Of mind, body and soul,
All my cares I share with You,
Keep me in Your fold.

You are my great healer
Your Word gives me peace,
You are my great healer
You bring me to my knees.

HIS WORD WILL LIFT YOU UP

Be kind to yourself
In all the ways you can,
Make Jesus your master
So you can spread His joy around.

You will have a loving heart,
Think twice before you speak,
You will walk on His path
Though ups and downs you meet.

The stress of life takes its toll,
Good and bad days come along,
But you know His holy Word
Is there to make you strong.

You can lean on Him forever,
His supplies never run out,
Accept His pure love today,
Never give in to doubt.

HE CARES FOR YOU

My pillow is Your shoulder
When cares fill my head,
I give them to You Lord
While I try to get some rest.

You will always see me right,
My faith tells me so,
I shouldn't doubt what You can do
There's nothing You don't know.

I have to focus on You Lord
To let my worries go,
I know You're always with me,
Your love to me You show.

Only You, almighty You
The precious King of Kings
Can take my cares away
When my heart to You I bring.

HIS LOVE IS ALL I KNOW

His love is all I know,
What joy fills my heart
When I talk to the Saviour,
Our love will never part.

His love is all I know
On this path I walk each day,
Hand in hand we go,
He leads me on my way.

His love is all I know
When I stand on shaky ground,
I state my case to Him,
My prayer is heaven bound.

His love is all I know
When peace commands my all,
I feel His joy divine,
I'm glad I heard His call.

GUIDE ME

Thank You dear One
For guiding me through my life,
Every day I have to meet You
To start the day off right.

You're there to share my joys
When I have a happy heart
And You guide me on the days
When I don't know where to start.

I just keep giving my cares
Up to You in prayer,
My faith and trust tell me
You take them all up there.

You know my heart's desire,
I feel Your love within,
Guide me all my days Lord,
Your love You always give.

FACE EACH DAY

Face each day
With hope in your heart,
His love and yours
Will never part.

Your day may be
Fast or slow,
But you can be sure
The Saviour knows.

Each turn and hill,
Valley and stream,
Whatever the way,
On Him you can lean.

Pray for each other
Along the way,
His blessings will come
To face each day.

SILENT CONVERSATION

HE IS DEVOTED TO YOU...

"For where two or three come together in my name, I am with them".

Matthew 18 : 20

FEED YOUR FAITH

Feed your faith and nourish it
With His gracious Words,
You'll find His love and teachings
In His Book to serve.

Invite Him to your side
In everything you choose,
Let Him be the centre
Of your life in all you do.

Feed your faith
By reading His Holy Word,
The blue print of life
That we must observe.

For happiness forever
Read His Holy Word,
The food for your soul
That it so deserves.

HOLY SPIRIT LOVE

When I feel Your Spirit near,
My soul shines inside,
That's why I'm so glad
Within me You abide.

It can be just a second,
I feel perfect love,
I know I've been touched
By Holy Spirit love.

No matter what I'm doing
Or wherever I am,
When Your Spirit comes near
I want to take His Holy hand.

So thank You precious Lord
For Your Spirit who lives with us,
Eternal thanks to Him
For the way He brings Your love.

REFLECTION

Reflect His love in all you do,
His light will shine through you,
Bearing His sweet reflection
On those He sends to you.

Reflect His calm every day
No matter what comes your way,
Don't let the storm clouds brew,
Call on His calm that's what you do.

Be a mirror image of His grace
Because one day you will see His face,
A loving heart He'll give to you,
Reflect His love, He needs you to.

HIS GREATEST BLESSING

His greatest blessing is
His Holy Spirit I know,
Bringing His gift of love
Because He loves us so.

Many times through life,
You'll feel His Spirit near,
Showering His love on you
To wash away your fears.

There will still be ups and downs
As you travel life's road,
But His Comforter is with you,
In you He's made His home.

So when you call Jesus
To live in your heart,
The change in you is miraculous,
You will make a new start.

MY QUIET TIME

I love this time Lord
When my soul can rest,
My chores for the day are done,
I come to be blessed.

I give You thanks Dear One
For guidance through my day,
Your strength and protection
Is with me along the way.

Weary I close my eyes for sleep,
I call You to my side,
Your reassurance comes to me
To shield me through the night.

Then when I awake
Your morning melodies I hear,
Dawn is fresh and new
As again I call You near.

So in my quiet time Lord
Shroud me in Your peace,
I feel Your arms around me
My Saviour You'll always be.

FORGIVE TO RECEIVE

Forgive a hurt that's done to you,
Strange though it seems,
You will be paid in full
By the Saviour who sees.

Humanity just can't reason
With a task that seems too big,
But when you know the Master,
Forgiveness can be reached.

In Jesus you can forgive,
Though the heart will struggle to see,
But in His great love,
When you forgive you will receive.

When you forgive a wrong
Your reward is a hundred fold,
You will receive in full measure,
In His Word it is told.

HELP ME UNDERSTAND YOU…

"We cannot understand the great things he does, and to his miracles there is no end."

Job 9 : 10

GLIMPSE OF HOPE

Serving You, helping others
To see a glimpse of hope,
Though a light grows dim,
Give me strength to cope.

I don't know where to put
My next step ahead,
Fear rises up inside,
My tears I have to shed.

Give me a glimpse of hope Lord
As I try to work this out,
Stay by my side,
Dispel my hurts and doubts.

Help me to put my trust
In the words that You spoke
Many years ago Lord,
To be my glimpse of hope.

RAINBOW'S WONDER

The wonder of the rainbow
Still draws me in awe,
Her sight is so amazing,
Each time I love her more.

When she appears
I see His glory shine,
Colours made in heaven
Thrill this heart of mine.

So graceful she looks
As she spans the open sky,
Reaching so perfectly
From side to side.

Her colours are a wonder
To give thrill and peace,
Makes you search your soul,
One day her maker you will meet!

SHOW HIS LOVE

To be touched by His Spirit
And be part of the family of Christ,
To transpire others lives
And walk in His light.

By showing His love
You can change others too,
His love in you abides,
That's what they see in you.

And so it passes on,
From one life to the next,
His Holy Spirit will shine,
For you to be your best.

So you can show His love
And think of your fellow man,
He depends on you
To make His Holy stand.

LOVE AND GRACE FOR ALL

In His eyes we are His children,
How precious each one is,
We are His beloved,
We belong to Him.

He asks for simple faith
To believe in His great love,
So you will know His grace,
A gift for everyone.

His love and grace abide
In the Holy Trinity,
Profound pure love
That came from Calvary.

Take His love and grace,
Be filled with joy divine,
Your soul will be renewed
In His appointed time.

COVER ME WITH YOUR WINGS

Cover me with Your wings Lord,
Protect me all the time,
Keep me safe all my days,
Always be mine.

Cover me with Your wings Lord
And bring Your love divine,
Fill my soul to overflow,
Join Your heart to mine.

Cover me with Your wings Lord
So I feel You close to me,
Though the world crowds me in
Your presence will set me free.

Cover me with Your wings Lord
So Your light will always shine
On me as I journey on,
Always be mine.

HIS QUIET VOICE

In the quiet times
He is always there,
Though His voice is quiet,
For you He always cares.

It's living in His love
That is so profound to me,
He is ever true,
Every day He walks with me.

So whether His voice is quiet,
It's always there indeed,
I just have to be patient
For His will to come to me.

RICH IN CHRIST

To be rich in Christ,
You only have to believe
In the Prince of Peace
Who gave us Calvary.

To be rich in Christ
Means He will dwell in your heart
To bring you joy untold,
From you He'll never part.

Unlike earthly riches,
The Saviour gives His wealth,
It's measured by your kindness,
The way you can help.

So to be rich in Christ,
Spread His message around,
He sees all you do,
In Him you're safe and sound.

BOW AT HIS THRONE

Bow at His Throne
When you want to meet the King,
He is the Lord Almighty,
He demands your everything.

You can lay your heart's desire
At His holy feet,
Only if it's in His plan,
Will it come to be.

Bow at His Throne
For a serve of love divine,
You will receive in full measure
In His fullness of time.

Bow at His Throne
Where His blessings flow,
His pure love will shower you,
His Spirit you will know.

THE TWISTS AND TURNS OF LIFE

Life takes us on a journey
Sometimes long, sometimes short,
The Saviour travels with us
Through our daily walks.

Many times we may get lost
Or can't see our way ahead,
But if we call on Jesus
The road we both will share.

You'll never do a "U" turn,
Going back just can't be done,
Keep your eyes on the Saviour,
God's precious Holy Son.

So in the twists and turns of life,
Share each journey with Him,
Whether high or low, rough or smooth,
On life's road, follow Him.

HEALING BALM

The pain in this world
Makes me write,
To help heal the scars
That have left their bite.

The wound will mend
And may leave a mark,
But the Saviour's love
Is healing balm.

Emotional scars can leave
A lifetime of pain,
The soothing balm of the Saviour
Will take the scars away.

He forgave us at Calvary,
Though His palms bear the mark,
So the least we can do
Is find forgiveness in our heart.

TWO BECOME ONE

The Saviour calls His children
To be sons and daughters of the King,
Nothing is impossible,
When you open your heart to Him.

What joy will own your soul
When you say "yes" to the King,
Gifts of grace and love
To your heart He will bring.

You will know His perfect peace
That will carry you all your days,
When two become one
Your joy will never fade.

Two become one
When you open your heart's door
To receive the gift of Jesus,
You will live forever more.

ETERNAL SPRING

Drink from His eternal spring,
Receive His gifts for life,
Your joy will overflow
From He who makes things right.

He desires your commitment
For truth, love and grace,
These gifts He freely gives
To those who see in faith.

His eternal spring will sparkle
With gifts He longs to give,
Wisdom, strength and peace
For all who believe in Him.

So drink from His eternal spring
To live forever more,
Accept His gift of love
When He knocks on your heart's door!

PART THREE

Jesus answered, "Love the Lord your God
with all your heart, with all your soul,
and with all your mind."

Matthew 22 : 37

LEAN ON HIM…

"…I made you and will care for you;
I will give you help and rescue you."

Isaiah 46 : 4

A SPECIAL PURPOSE

There's nothing you can't do Lord,
You are the King of Kings,
Your wisdom is almighty,
Far beyond our understanding.

Your knowledge is supreme,
You made the universe,
For each wondering soul
You have a special purpose.

All our heart's desires
Must claim Your ownership,
To bring them to Your Throne
To accept Your love and live.

Each special purpose of Yours
You give so tenderly,
It will all come to pass
The how and why we will see.

SPEAK TO MY SOUL LORD

Thank You for Your love Lord
That speaks in every way,
An eternal spring that flows,
That showers me every day.

You are so devoted
To hearts that welcome You in,
You speak to each soul
That's where Your home is.

What joy fills it so,
Knowing You are there,
On my rainy days,
My cares we both will share.

So speak to my soul Lord,
Your Words come from eternity,
You have my life planned,
I bow on bended knee.

HIS WILL BE DONE

Whenever I want to talk Lord,
You are there,
Your ear always open
To hear my changing cares.

You never get tired
Of my requests,
You patiently deal with them
With a "no" or a "yes".

But for me my lesson is time,
I must wait and see what comes,
You have Your reasons Lord,
Your will not mine, be done.

ALL IN HIS APPOINTED TIME

All in His appointed time
Is paramount to me,
He has my journey planned,
My future He can see.

All in His appointed time
Things will come to pass,
For His strength to see it through,
I only have to ask.

All in His appointed time
I put my trust in Him,
He will lead me on my way
Though confusion reigns within.

My faith tells me to follow Him
And to ask for peace and calm,
For in knowing Him
He will send His soothing balm.

ASK

Ask Him to take your cares,
He will deal with them,
Put your trust in the Prince of Peace,
Let go and cling to Him.

Ask for His eternal love
To hold you while you share
Those inner fears that rise inside,
To the one who truly cares.

Ask for His watchful eye
To keep His gaze on you,
To equip you for the future,
That you will pass through.

Ask for His powerful arms
That He raised to stop the wind,
To always be around you,
With His peace He longs to give.

Ask so you'll receive,
This He promised so,
Whisper your prayers to Him,
He surely loves you so.

STRENGTH TO BE HAPPY

Give me the strength to be happy Lord
Though some days I just can't smile,
Show Your love to me
As I journey through the miles.

Shine Your beam of light
On me to give me warmth,
That brings Your Spirit near
With comforting thoughts.

Show me Your Word Lord,
That can lift me high above,
Feelings of fear and doubt
To Your everlasting love.

Your love, the only love,
That will give me happiness
And the strength to abide
Within Your Holiness.

GOD'S PLANS…
THE BEST PLANS…

"I alone know the plans I have for you,
plans to bring you prosperity…"

Jeremiah 29 : 11

WHAT'S BEST FOR ME

You always know what's best for me
Though many days may pass,
I don't know what to do or say
When I carry a heavy heart.

Sometimes it seems a life-time
Before a change appears,
But then I see the sunshine
Which dries away my tears.

In prayer I give my heart
To the King of Kings above,
All things are made possible
When I turn to Him for love.

He always knows what's best for me,
So patient I must be,
At His appointed time,
His plan will come to me.

PEARLS OF LIGHT

Listen to your soul
For inward peace,
Reach for God's Word
To feel complete.

The challenges of life
Will weigh on your mind
But if you seek God's help,
Pearls of light you will find.

Your actions will reflect
How you feel inside,
Within His pearls of light
With you He will reside.

Look into your soul
It reveals the truth,
It holds His pearls of light
That His Spirit brings to you.

Look into your soul
That holds His pearls of light,
They will reflect on your heart
To make your life so bright!

YOUR LOVE, MY LOVE

Your love, my love,
Equals pure love,
Your radiance spreading far and near
From Your Throne above.

It overflows my soul
And fills me to the brim,
With Your precious joy and peace,
That only You can give.

You are heaven's light,
You shine eternally,
Your Spirit lives amongst us,
To remind us of Thee.

Moments of wonder
You surely give to me,
Your love, my love,
Will blend eternally.

YOUR WORDS

Thank You Lord for Your Words
That are forever true,
They live within us,
We are made new in You.

Your Words fill our hearts
To follow Your ways
And change us in Your image,
To live all our days.

Your Words bring us calm
When we need inner peace,
To remind us of our duty
To help someone in need.

Your Words fill my soul
And guide my heart inside
Like a beam of light to show,
Your Words will last through time.

THE SACRED SOUL

The sacred soul so secret,
Your connection to the Lord,
Commit your life to Him
Because it's you He adores.

The world cannot spoil it,
Or tarnish its core,
Where the Holy Spirit dwells
To love you more and more.

He will show you God's ways
But most of all His love,
That He showers all over you,
So His Disciple you will become.

A cleansing so pure
Will possess your soul,
You will shine on the inside,
That will make you whole.

The never failing love of Christ
Will never let you go,
His rewards will be many
Because His love you will show.

TRUST, FAITH AND BELIEF

Believe in the King of Kings,
For inner trust to reside,
Inside your heart of hearts
Your fears you can push aside.

With faith in your heart
You can follow your dreams,
He wants to give you the best
So you can succeed.

The Saviour knows what's in your heart
He wants to supply your need,
As He knows what's best for you,
Just trust your faith and believe.

PART FOUR

"…he never said a word.
He was arrested and sentenced and led off to die,
and no one cared about his fate…"

Isaiah 53 : 7, 8

SILENT CONVERSATION

BETRAYED...
FOR THIRTY SILVER COINS...

"Then one of the twelve disciples – the one named Judas Iscariot – went to the chief priests and asked, "What will you give me if I betray Jesus to you?" They counted out thirty silver coins and gave them to him."

Matthew 26 : 14, 15

IN THE SHADOWS OF THE OLIVE GROVE

In the shadows of the Olive Grove
Weary eyes surrender to sleep,
While the Master close-by
Prayed so earnestly.

The reason for His birth
Was a pending sacrifice,
Now approaching fast
For the sins of all mankind.

In the shadows of the Olive Grove
Soldiers came in search,
A kiss that would betray Him
For a pouch of silvers worth.

His ministry now complete,
As prophecy would come to be
As He was led away for trial,
He made His way to Calvary.

In the shadows of the Olive Grove
He held the world in His hands,
Our redemption was nigh,
A Cross would claim the Son of Man!

EASTER LOVE

Easter love came calling
On a hill at Calvary,
Two thousand years ago
To set all people free.

Easter love was planned
Many years before that day,
As prophesied in the Bible
A Saviour would come to save.

From twelve years old He preached "the Word"
But many disbelieved,
How could this child from Nazareth
Be God's Holy seed?

So, thank You Lord for Easter love,
You bore our sins up high,
Your heavenly Father raised You
To give us eternal life.

PIERCED HANDS

Pierced hands stretched forth
In want reaching for you,
Calling for you tenderly
So your heart He can renew.

Pierced hands stretched forth
Longing for your attention,
And eyes that hold pure love
Long for your acceptance.

Pierced hands will carry
You through every day,
Though you can't see Him,
He's there in every way.

His pierced hands will heal
The deepest hurt or scar,
With His balm He will anoint you,
You will never see the mark.

So thank You for Your precious hands
That always want to held
Me close as close,
As in days of old.

EASTER MORNING...
ETERNAL JOY...

"Look at my hands and my feet,
and see that it is I myself…"

Luke 24 : 39

THANK YOU FOR CALVARY

Thank You Lord for Your love
That You lay on me,
Thank You for Calvary,
You died to set me free.

Your heavenly Father lifted You,
To life You rose for man,
You are the great Redeemer,
We must seek Your pierced hand.

Now guide us on our way,
You live to show Your love,
You walk with us each day
From Your heaven above.

Your love so powerful
It took my sin away,
Thank You for Calvary,
You rose; You live today!

HOLY SPIRIT

Holy Spirit, hold my hand
Give me strength to face today,
My world feels upside down
Now show me how to pray.

Holy Spirit, soothe my soul,
Shroud me in Your peace and calm,
My heart feels You speak
As You anoint me in Your balm.

Holy Spirit, I hear Your voice
To prompt my daily path,
You go ahead before me
Like a lantern in the dark.

Holy Spirit, God's precious gift
Who comforts and heals my soul,
You bring His love completely,
Now You have made me whole.

Holy Spirit, You shine forever,
You belong to the Trinity,
Father, Son and Holy Spirit
Will always live in me.

JESUS...
THE ONLY GIFT FOR EVERYONE...

"She gave birth to her first son,
wrapped him in cloths and laid him in a manger -
there was no room for them to stay in the inn."

Luke 2 : 7

A PRICELESS LIFE

He was born under
The Star of the East
And the wonder of angels
Who declared His birth in peace.

The shepherds in the fields
Saw this glorious site
Of the angels who told them
Of His birth that night.

He would grow into a man
Who could walk on the sea,
He could touch and heal,
This man from Galilee.

Down through the ages
This priceless life stands out,
His awe and His wonder
We cannot live without.

One priceless life
Called "The Nazarene",
One so perfect
Will again be seen!

THIS BABY BOY

Christmas time so special,
God's great gift to the world,
The birth of the Saviour
His story we have to tell.

Not all mankind receives
A gift under the tree
But Jesus is our gift
Who brings us Eternity.

The night sky brought the angels
Who sang of glory and joy,
The arrival of the Saviour,
God's own Son, this baby boy!

This baby boy so special
With miracles to unfold,
Would grow to be the Saviour
For mankind to behold.

Yes the humble stable in Bethlehem
Brought forth God's only Son,
This night sacred forever
Given by God above.

ANGELS BROUGHT JOY

Angels brought joy
On the first Christmas night,
The Messiah is born
Under the Star so bright.

A phenomenon in the sky,
The angels proclaimed
God's gift of His Son,
"Jesus" would be His name!

Even the sheep and the cattle
Bowed down that Holy night,
To worship the baby King
On this holy site.

All Heaven applauded
When baby Jesus was born,
Mary safely delivered
God's precious baby boy.

In wonder and awe
She cradled Him so,
Believing this miracle
Will forever be known!

STAR OF THE EAST

A guide so vivid in the sky,
Star of the East shines bright
For the Wisemen on their way
For Bethlehem's Holy night.

Glorious praise from the angels came down
With glory and joy from above,
To the shepherds in the fields
God's gift; a baby boy bringing love.

Loving parents overwhelmed
At this miracle that night,
The Star of the East shone down
To proclaim this heavenly sight.

Star of the East, a guide
Illumed the Manger from above,
Baby Jesus delivered by Mary,
The Saviour of the world has come!

ALSO BY CLAIRE GROSE

ABOUT THE AUTHOR

Claire worked as a Government Public Servant in the Lands Department, Adelaide, South Australia until she married and became a mother of two boys.

She later returned to the work force during which time she gained a "Living Hope" Phone Counselling certificate which influenced her need to help others.

Through this and personal experience she found herself inspired by God's love to put pen to paper.

PHOTO CREDITS

Cover photo: Stained glass window: Salisbury Uniting Church, used by permission.
Page 2: Angaston rose garden, S.A. – Claire Grose
Page 12: Wattle Tree, Tanunda – Claire Grose
Page 24: Belladonna Lillies, Williamstown, S.A. – Claire Grose
Page 31: Ducklings, Fremont Park, S.A. – Claire Grose
Page 39: Canola field, Blakeview Heights, S.A. – Claire Grose
Page 47: Winter Trees, Tanunda, S.A. – Claire Grose
Page 55: Rainbow Lorikeets, Gorge Wildlife Park, S.A. – Claire Grose, used by permission.
Page 70: Footbridge, Fremont Park, Elizabeth, S.A. . – Claire Grose
Page 78: Autmn vineyards, Angaston, S.A. – Claire Grose
Page 87: Olive Grove, Elizabeth, S.A., - Claire Grose
Page 92: Stained Glass Window, Salisbury Uniting Church, S.A. – Claire Grose
Page 96: Glowing candle – Claire Grose

SILENT CONVERSATION

www.ingramcontent.com/pod-product-compliance
Lightning Source LLC
Chambersburg PA
CBHW051539010526
44107CB00064B/2785